A Community Shakespeare Company
Edition of

THE TWO GENTLEMEN OF VERONA

Original verse adaptation by

Richard Carter

"Enriching young lives, cultivating community"

Other original verse adaptations by Richard Carter,
available through iUniverse:

As You Like It

The Comedy Of Errors

The Taming Of The Shrew

A Community Shakespeare Company
Edition of

THE TWO GENTLEMEN OF VERONA

Original verse adaptation by
Richard Carter

"Enriching young lives, cultivating community"

iUniverse, Inc.
New York Lincoln Shanghai

A Community Shakespeare Company Edition of
THE TWO GENTLEMEN OF VERONA

Copyright © 2007 by Richard R. Carter, Jr.

iUniverse books may be ordered through booksellers or by contacting:

iUniverse
2021 Pine Lake Road, Suite 100
Lincoln, NE 68512
www.iuniverse.com
1-800-Authors (1-800-288-4677)

Because of the dynamic nature of the Internet, any Web addresses or links contained in this book may have changed since publication and may no longer be valid.

ISBN: 978-0-595-45825-7 (pbk)
ISBN: 978-0-595-90125-8 (ebk)

Printed in the United States of America

CONTENTS

A NOTE ABOUT THE SONG IN THE PLAY

A tune for "Who is Sylvia can be found in "Shakespeare's Songbook", by Ross W. Duffin, pub. W.W. Norton & Co., NY, NY, 2004. The original tune has been lost, and the book's author chose another tune with a similar phrase and metric structure. It was commonplace in Shakespeare's time to set new words to an old song. Shakespeare does not specify who sings, "Who Is Sylvia"—it may be Proteus, or one of the musicians—but in this adaptation it is implied that Proteus is the singer.

CAST OF CHARACTERS

VALENTINE
PROTEUS   the two gentlemen of Verona

JULIA   loved by Proteus
SILVIA   loved by Valentine

SPEED   servant to Valentine
LANCE   servant to Proteus
LUCETTA   servant to Julia

ANTONIO   father to Proteus
PANTINO   servant to Antonio

DUKE OF MILAN   Silvia's father
TURIO   suitor to Silvia
EGLAMOUR   a knight who helps Silvia escape

HOST OF THE INN   at Milan

OUTLAW 1
OUTLAW 2   three of the band who elect Valentine their leader
OUTLAW 3

MUSICIANS
SERVANTS

(This play should run approximately 90 minutes without intermission)

ACT I, scene 1

VALENTINE
Cease to persuade me, Proteus, my loving friend;
Home-keeping youth have homely wits in the end.
But since thou lov'st, love still, and thrive therein;
Though you live dully at home, I'm sure 'tis no sin.

PROTEUS
Wilt thou be gone? Sweet Valentine, adieu.
Think on thy Proteus as no less happy than you.
And in thy danger, if ever danger do enfold thee,
Commend thyself to my prayers, for in them I'll hold thee.

VALENTINE
Wilt thou pray for my success on a love-book, friend?

PROTEUS
Upon some book I love I'll pray, and there's an end.

VALENTINE
Love is your master: he masters you with the promise of earthly delights.
One fading moment's mirth is bought with twenty tedious nights.

PROTEUS
'Tis Love you cavil at, I am not Love.

VALENTINE
I think you are Love's tool.

PROTEUS
So, by your circumstance, you would call your Proteus a fool.

VALENTINE
Methinks you are so yoked, you should not be chronicled for wise.
I waste my time to counsel you, Signore Googly Eyes.
Once more adieu. My father at the road expects my coming,
There to see me shipped; I can hear his fingers drumming.

PROTEUS
All happiness to thee in Milan, Valentine; keep you well.

VALENTINE
As much to you at home, Proteus, and so farewell.

(EXIT VALENTINE)

PROTEUS
He after honor hunts, I after love.
He leaves his friends to dignify them, as he'll soon prove.
I leave my self, my friends, and all to burn at love's stake.
Thou, Julia, hast metamorphosed me: I give all for thy sweet sake.

(ENTER SPEED)

SPEED
Sir Proteus, save you! Saw you my master hither?

PROTEUS
But now he parted for Milan; you may yet find him thither.

SPEED
Twenty to one he is shipped, and in losing him I have played the sheep.

PROTEUS
Indeed, a sheep doth often stray for want of his Bo-Peep.

SPEED
You conclude I am the sheep, and my master is the shepherd?
That I can deny if I'm worth my salt.

PROTEUS
I think your salt is peppered.

SPEED
The shepherd seeks the sheep, not the other way around;
I seek my master, he seeks not me: therefore is my reason sound.

PROTEUS
The sheep for fodder follows the shepherd; the shepherd follows not for food.
Thou followest for wages, therefore thou art a sheep.

SPEED
Don't be rude.
Such another proof will make me cry, "baa."

PROTEUS
Gave'st thou Julia my letter?

SPEED
Ay, sir: I, a lost mutton, gave it to her, a mutton's debtor,
And she, a laced mutton, gave me *nothing* for my pain.

PROTEUS
Here's too little pasture for so many muttons.

SPEED
Then slaughter *her*, I'm too thin from so little gain.

PROTEUS
You have a quick wit.

SPEED
And yet my quick wit cannot overtake your slow purse.

PROTEUS
Come, come: what said she?

SPEED
Must I bear with you? This is getting worse and worse.

PROTEUS
Pray, open the matter; tell me, and be brief.

SPEED
Pray, open your purse: let money and matter grant us both relief.

PROTEUS
(GIVES HIM A COIN) Well, here's for your pains. What said she?

SPEED
I think you'll hardly win her.
I couldn't win enough from her to buy my dinner!
For delivering your letter, she gave me not so much as a ducat.

PROTEUS
What said she?

SPEED
Nothing. She's hard as steel, cold as an old iron bucket.
Henceforth you may carry your letters yourself; I'll commend you to my master.

(EXIT SPEED)

PROTEUS
Be gone! I'll find some other way to mend this present disaster.
I fear my Julia would not read my lines, receiving them from this worthless post.
I must send some better messenger, or else my bread is toast!

(EXIT PROTEUS)

ACT I, scene 2

(VERONA. JULIA'S GARDEN. ENTER JULIA AND LUCETTA)

JULIA
Do you counsel me to fall in love, Lucetta? Say, now we're alone.

LUCETTA
Aye, madam, truly; if heedful seeds are sown.

JULIA
Of all the fair gentlemen that with talk encounter me,
Which is worthiest of love? I would have thy opinion of thee.

LUCETTA
If you please, repeat their names and I'll show you my mind,
According to my shallow skill, to tell cat from kind.

JULIA
What think you of Sir Eglamour?

LUCETTA
As of a knight, fair, neat and fine;
But were I you, though he's well spoken, he should never be mine.

JULIA
What think you of rich Mercatio?

LUCETTA
Well of his wealth; of himself, so-so

JULIA
And of the gentle Proteus?

LUCETTA
Lord, madam, 'tis a shame to continue this show!
Who am I, unworthy body, to censure lovely gentlemen thus?

JULIA
Why not on Proteus, as all the rest? Why on him make such a fuss?

LUCETTA
Then so: of many good men, I would say I think him best.

JULIA
Your reason?

LUCETTA
Faith, gentle madam, you put me to the test.
I have none but a woman's reason: I think him so because I think him so.

JULIA
Wouldst thou have me cast my love on him?

LUCETTA
I say you go girl, go!

JULIA
Why, he of all the rest? I cannot say he moves me.

LUCETTA
Yet he of all the rest, I think, best loves ye.

JULIA
His little speaking shows his love but small.

LUCETTA
Fire closest kept burns most of all.

JULIA
I would I knew his mind.

LUCETTA
(GIVES A LETTER) Then do but read this letter.

JULIA
(READS) "To Julia." Say, from whom?

LUCETTA
The contents will show you better.

JULIA
Who gave it thee?

LUCETTA
Sir Valentine's page, and sent from Proteus, I think.

JULIA
And you presume to receive it? You put my modesty on the brink!
Dare you to harbor wanton lines, and conspire against my youth?
Take the paper, see it returned, or I'll see thee no more in truth.

LUCETTA
To plead for love, I think, deserves more fee than hate.

JULIA
Will you be gone?

LUCETTA
Aye, will I, that you may ruminate.

(EXIT LUCETTA)

JULIA
And yet I would I had read it. Fie! I cannot call her back now,
And ask for what I scolded her for! Peace, Julia: don't have a cow.
She should know that I, as a maid, in modesty must say no,
Which she should construe as "yes." O, why didn't I just say so?
My penance is to call her back, and ask remission for my folly.
What ho! Lucetta!

(ENTER LUCETTA WITH A LETTER)

LUCETTA
What would you? (DROPS THE LETTER.) Oops, I dropped something. Oh, golly.
(SHE TAKES UP THE LETTER AGAIN.)

JULIA
What was it you took up so gingerly?

LUCETTA
Nothing.

JULIA
Has the dinner been laid?

LUCETTA
I would it had, that you might kill your stomach on your meat, and not your maid.

JULIA
Sweet Lucetta: why didst thou stoop?

LUCETTA
To pick up a paper I let fall.

JULIA
And is that paper nothing?

LUCETTA
Nothing concerning me, that's all.

JULIA
Pray let it lie.

LUCETTA
It cannot lie, unless the reader be false.

JULIA
Has some love of yours writ you a song in rhyme?

LUCETTA
Guess again.

JULIA
Nay, what else?
Let's see your song.
(LUCETTA WITHHOLDS THE LETTER)
How now, minion! Your note is too saucy.

LUCETTA
And your tune is flat.

JULIA
You shall mar all else with your unruly singing.

LUCETTA
(YIELDING THE LETTER) 'Tis from Proteus, I told you that.

JULIA
(LOOKS INTO IT) O! Here is a declaration of love. No more! I must not look!
(SHE TEARS THE LETTER INTO PIECES)

LUCETTA
Saints have mercy! Madam, forbear: you're acting like a kook!
(SHE TRIES TO COLLECT THE PIECES.)

JULIA
Go, get you gone, let the papers lie. You'd be fingering them to annoy me!

LUCETTA
(ASIDE) She'd fain be "annoyed" in private; it's no picnic being her employee.

(EXIT LUCETTA)

JULIA
O hateful hands, to tear loving words! I'll kiss each piece for amends.
(SHE COLLECTS SOME OF THE FRAGMENTS)
Here is"kind Julia," there "Love-wounded Proteus;" what shall I make of these odds and ends?
Here his name is writ twice: "Forlorn Proteus, passionate Proteus;" aye, me!
"To the sweet Julia," is in the very same line: he couples us so prettily.
Thus will I fold us, one upon another: now kiss, and do what you will.

(ENTER LUCETTA)

LUCETTA
Madam! Dinner is ready!

JULIA
Must you be so shrill?

LUCETTA
What, shall these papers yet lie, and remain like telltales here?

JULIA
If you respect them, take them up. Don't leave them lying there.

LUCETTA
I was taken up for laying them down, then put down for picking them up.

JULIA
I know you have a liking for them: you may collect them while I go sup.

LUCETTA
Madam, you may say what sights you see; I see things too.

JULIA
Come, come, you saucy girl: will it please you go?

(EXEUNT)

ACT I, scene 3

(VERONA. ANTONIO'S HOUSE. ENTER ANTONIO AND PANTINO)

ANTONIO
Tell me, Pantino, what sad talk was that,
Wherein my brother held you of late?

PANTINO
'Twas of Proteus, your son, who seems never to roam;
Your brother wondered that you would let him stay at home,
While other men put forth their sons to seek fortune and fame:
Some to universities, some to the wars to make their name;
Others travel to discover islands far away.
He said Proteus was meet for this, and he hoped I might sway
You, to let your son spend no more time upon this stage,
Which, says your brother, is impeachment to his age.

ANTONIO
Nor need'st thou much importune me to that
Whereon I've been hammering: it's time we had a chat.
For I have considered well his loss of time;
Not being tutored in the world his crime.
He cannot be a perfect man if I bow to his whim;
Tell me whither you think it best I send him?

PANTINO
I think your lordship knows how Valentine, his companion,
Attends the court at Milan, where the Duke holds dominion.

ANTONIO
I know it well.

PANTINO
Then I think it were good you send him there,
To converse with noblemen everywhere,
And practice every exercise worthy of his youth.

ANTONIO
I like thy counsel; thou hast spoken the truth.
And that you may perceive how well I listen,
To the court I will dispatch him with the speediest expedition.

PANTINO
Tomorrow, may it please you, Don Alphonso sets forth
To salute the Duke with other gentlemen of good worth.

ANTONIO
Good company, and with them Proteus shall go,
And in good time, for here he comes now!

(ENTER PROTEUS, MUSING ON A LETTER)

PROTEUS
Sweet love, sweet lines! Here is love's dart:
Here is her hand, the agent of her heart!

ANTONIO
How now? What letter have you there?

PROTEUS
Letter? What letter? Oh, *this* letter here.
May't please your lordship, 'tis a word or two
From Valentine, delivered by a friend who came through.

ANTONIO
Lend me the letter: let me see what news.

PROTEUS
There is none, my lord; merely his views
On how happily he lives, how well loved he is,
And daily graced by the Duke; what good fortune is his.
He wishes me with him, partner of his bliss.

ANTONIO
And how stand *you* affected by this?

PROTEUS
As one relying on your will, not depending on his wish.

ANTONIO
His desire and my will together share the same dish.
Muse not that I thus suddenly proceed:
I am resolved you shall join him, and depart with speed.
With Valentine, in the imperious court
Thou shalt spend some time, in study and sport.
Tomorrow be in readiness to go,

PROTEUS
But father, why?

ANTONIO
Because I say so.

PROTEUS
My lord, I cannot so soon be provided.

ANTONIO
What you want shall be sent after; I've already decided.
Tomorrow thou must go, there's no other condition.
Come Pantino; you shall be employed to hasten his expedition.

(EXEUNT ANTONIO AND PANTINO)

PROTEUS
I shunned the fire for fear the meat would be browned,
And drenched me in the sea where I am drowned!
I feared to show my father Julia's letter,
Lest he disapprove, and in so doing, fetter
Our certain happiness, now uncertain as an April day
Which first shows the sun, and by and by, a cloud takes all away.

(ENTER PANTINO)

PANTINO
Sir Proteus, your father calls. He is in haste; I pray you go.

PROTEUS
My heart accords, and yet a thousand times it answers "no."

(EXEUNT)

ACT II, scene 1

(MILAN. THE DUKE'S PALACE. ENTER SILVIA: LETS HER GLOVE DROP, EXITS. ENTER VALENTINE AND SPEED)

SPEED
Sir, your glove! (PICKS IT UP.)

VALENTINE
Not mine, my gloves are on.

SPEED
Why then this may be yours, for this is but one.

VALENTINE
Ha, let me see. Aye, give it me, it's mine.
Ah, Silvia, Silvia! Sweet ornament that decks a thing divine!
Do you know Madam Silvia?

SPEED
She that your worship doth love?

VALENTINE
How do you know?

SPEED
By these marks, and by them your love I'll prove:
You were wont, when you laughed, to crow like a cock; when you walked, you walked like a lion;
When you were sad, it was for want of money. Now you're transformed, there's no denyin'.
You have learnt, like Sir Proteus, to walk alone, like one that has the plague;
To sigh like a schoolboy, to weep like a wench, your brains are mixed like a scrambled egg.
You relish a love-song like a robin redbreast, you watch like one who fears robbing,
Speak puling like a beggar at Hallowmas. When I see you, I can scarce keep from sobbing.

VALENTINE
Are all these things perceived in me?

SPEED
Like a malady for which there's no curin'.
Your follies shine through so every eye can perceive, like a physician examining your urine.

VALENTINE
But dost thou know my lady Silvia?

SPEED
She that you gaze on at supper?

VALENTINE
Hast thou observed that? Is she not well favored?

SPEED
I'd call her a fixer-upper.

VALENTINE
I have loved her since I saw her, and still I see her fair.

SPEED
If you love her you cannot see her. (KNOCKS ON VALENTINE'S HEAD) Anyone home in there?

VALENTINE
Why cannot I see her?

SPEED
Because Love is blind. O that you had my vision!
Where are the eyes that shone on Sir Proteus when *he* was the object of your derision?

VALENTINE
What should I see then?

SPEED
Your own present folly, for like him, you cannot garter your hose;
A man cannot see to tie his stockings when a woman has him by the nose.

VALENTINE
Then *you* must be in love, for this morning, you could not see to wipe my shoes.

SPEED

I was in love with my bed. And for that you beat me; Sir, I've paid my dues.

VALENTINE

In conclusion, I stand affected to her. She asked me to write some lines
To one she loves, so I've writ this letter. I know not for whom she pines.

SPEED

Are they not lamely writ?

VALENTINE

No, boy, but as well as I can write them.
Here she comes.

(ENTER SILVIA)

SPEED

(ASIDE) O excellent motion! Now like her puppet will he recite them!

VALENTINE

Madam and mistress, a thousand good morrows.

SILVIA

Two thousand, Sir Valentine, to you.

SPEED

(ASIDE) See how she pays him interest. I'd like to invest in her too.

VALENTINE

As you enjoined me, I have writ your letter, to your secret, nameless friend.
(HE GIVES HER THE LETTER)

SILVIA

I thank you, gentle servant. (LOOKS AT THE LETTER) 'Tis well done, and
there's an end.

VALENTINE

I writ at random, very doubtfully, being ignorant to whom it goes.

SILVIA

Perchance you think it too much. Is this writing the cause of your woes?

VALENTINE
No, madam; please you command; I'll write it a thousand times o're.

SILVIA
(OFFERING TO RETURN THE LETTER) And yet take it again; henceforth, I'll trouble you no more.

VALENTINE
What means your ladyship? Do you not like it?

SILVIA
Yes, yes; it's quaintly writ.
But since unwillingly, take it back.

VALENTINE
It's for you.

SILVIA
Nay, not one bit.
The words are for you; I would have them writ more movingly.

VALENTINE
Then I'll cheerfully write another.

SILVIA
And when it's writ, *you* may take it, to pay yourself for the bother.

(EXIT SILVIA)

SPEED
(ASIDE) O excellent device, O jest unseen! Was there ever heard a better? That my master, being scribe, to *himself* should write the letter!

VALENTINE
How now, sir? Reasoning with yourself?

SPEED
Nay, rhyming; 'tis you have the reason.

VALENTINE
To do what?

SPEED
To be a spokesman for Madam Silvia. She woos you like a minx in season.

VALENTINE
She hath not writ me!

SPEED
What need she? She hath made *you* write to yourself.
Do you not see the jest?

VALENTINE
No, believe me.

SPEED
There's no believing you, sir; your wits are on the shelf.

VALENTINE
She gave me nothing, except an angry word.

SPEED
She hath given you a letter.

VALENTINE
Writ to her friend.

SPEED
You are her friend. Ha! This gets better and better.
So often have you writ to her, she in modesty could not reply,
So hath taught her lover to write himself. Trust me: you're the guy.
Why muse you, sir? 'Tis dinner time.

VALENTINE
I have dined.

SPEED
But not on food.
You feed on air, like the chameleon. Come dine.

VALENTINE
I'm not in the mood.

SPEED

Harken sir, I am nourished by victuals, and cannot feed on Love;
I would fain have meat. O, be not like your mistress; be moved, be moved!

(EXEUNT)

ACT II, scene 2

(VERONA. JULIA'S HOUSE. ENTER PROTEUS AND JULIA)

PROTEUS
Have patience, gentle Julia.

JULIA
I must, where there is no cure.

PROTEUS
When I can, I will return.

JULIA
You'll return sooner, if your heart is pure.
(GIVES A RING) Keep this remembrance, for thy Julia's sake.

PROTEUS
We'll make exchange, if this ring you'll take. (GIVES A RING IN RETURN)

JULIA
And seal the bargain with a holy kiss.

PROTEUS
Here is my hand, and my vow is this:
When that hour comes that I sigh not for thy sake,
The next hour some foul mischance o'ertake
Me, and torment me for my love's forgetfulness!
My father awaits, answer not in thy distress;
Your tide of tears will stay me longer than I should;
Julia farewell, I would stay if I could.

(ENTER PANTINO.)

PANTINO
Sir Proteus, you are stayed for.

PROTEUS
Go; I come, I come.
Alas, this parting strikes poor lovers dumb.

(EXEUNT.)

ACT II, scene 3

(VERONA. NEAR LANCE'S HOUSE. ENTER LANCE, WEEPING, LEADING A DOG)

LANCE
'Twill be an hour ere I have done weeping;
All the Lances have this fault in our keeping.
I am going with Sir Proteus to the Imperial's court.
I think Crab, my dog, be the sourest sort
Of dog that lives: my mother wept, my father wailed, my sister, how she cried;
Our maid howling, our cat wringing her hands. you'd think that I had died.
Yet this cruel-hearted cur shed not one tear.
He's a stone, with no more pity in him than a dog. (TO CRAB) Dost thou hear?
(TO THE AUDIENCE.) Nay, I'll show you the manner of it. (TAKES OFF HIS SHOE.) This shoe is my father.
No, this shoe is my mother. Nay, that cannot be neither.
Yes, it is! For it has the worser sole;
This shoe is my mother: the one with the hole.
And *this* one my father. This staff is my sister, for she is white as a lily.
This hat is Nan, our maid, and I am the dog. No, that's silly.
The dog is himself, and *I* am the dog. No, the dog is *me*. Aye, so.
Now come I to my father; (KNEELS) "Father, your blessing before I go."
Now the shoe cannot speak for weeping, so I kiss my father (KISSES SHOE), and he weeps on.
Now come I to kiss my mother (KISSES THE OTHER SHOE): that's my mother's breath up and down.
Now the dog all this while sheds not a tear, nor speaks a blessèd word.
But see how I lay the dust with my tears. I tell you, it's absurd.

(ENTER PANTINO)

PANTINO
Lance, away, away! Aboard! Thy master is shipped!
Away, ass, you'll lose the tide. If you tarry, you'll be whipped.

LANCE
It is no matter, for it is the unkindest tied that ever man tied.

PANTINO

What's the unkindest?

LANCE

Crab, my dog: he that's tied here beside
Me.

PANTINO

Tut, man, you'll lose thy voyage, and in doing so, lose thy master;
And in losing thy master, lose thy service, and in doing so cause a disaster.
Why dost thou stop my mouth?

LANCE

For fear thou shouldst lose thy tongue.

PANTINO

Where should I lose it?

LANCE

In thy tale.

PANTINO

In *thy* tail! Take that, you bum! (KICKS HIM)

LANCE

If the wind were down, I'd drive the boat with my sighs.

PANTINO

Come, man, wilt thou go?

LANCE

Sir, call me what thou wilt: I will follow, with Crab in tow.

(EXUENT)

ACT II, scene 4

(MILAN. THE DUKE'S PALACE. ENTER VALENTINE, SILVIA, TURIO, AND SPEED.)

SPEED
Master, Sir Turio frowns on you.

VALENTINE
Ay, boy, it is for love.

SPEED
Not of you, I think.

VALENTINE
Of my mistress.

SPEED
'Twere best you give him a shove.

(EXIT SPEED)

SILVIA
Servant, you are sad.

VALENTINE
I seem so.

TURIO
Seem you what you are not? So do counterfeits.

VALENTINE
So do *you*.

TURIO
What instance? What's your best shot?

VALENTINE
You *seem* wise.

TURIO
Instance to the contrary?

24

VALENTINE
Your folly.

TURIO
How quote you my folly?

VALENTINE
I quote it to your coat.

TURIO
My coat is a doublet.

VALENTINE
Double the fool!

SILVIA
Gentlemen, a fine volley,
But here comes my father, with a letter bearing news.

(ENTER DUKE, WITH A LETTER)

DUKE
Daughter Silvia, you are hard beset. Valentine, what say you to these views:
Which say your father is in health, and glad tidings come from your friends.

VALENTINE
I'm thankful to any happy messenger, and to all good news that he sends.

DUKE
Know ye Don Antonio?

VALENTINE
I know the gentleman to be of worth and estimation.

DUKE
Hath he not a son? Know you *him*?

VALENTINE
Aye, a son that well deserves his reputation.
I knew him as my self; from birth we spent our hours together,
And though *I* have been a truant, *he* hath made fair use of all weather.
Sir Proteus, for that's his name, is young, but his experience is old;

His head unmellowed, his judgment ripe, beyond his years, truth be told.
In a word, he is a gentleman, complete in feature and in mind.

DUKE
He is worthy of an empress' love, if all this I should find.
Well, he is come, and here means to spend his time awhile.
I think 'tis no unwelcome news; indeed, I see you smile.

VALENTINE
Should I have wished one thing, it is he.

DUKE
Then welcome him according to his worth:
Silvia, I speak to you, and you Turio, for Valentine has known him since birth.
I'll send him hither.

(EXIT DUKE)

VALENTINE
(TO SILVIA) This is the very gentleman I've often mentioned,
Who would have come along with me, for he was well-intentioned,
But that his mistress did hold his eyes locked in her crystal looks.

SILVIA
Then perchance she has freed them, and now, he studies love in books.

VALENTINE
Nay, I think she holds them still.

SILVIA
Then he should be blind. How could he seek you out?

VALENTINE
Why, lady, Love hath twenty pair of eyes.

TURIO
Spoken like a lout,
For they say, Valentine, that Love hath not an eye at all.

VALENTINE
'Tis well for you that upon even a homely object, Love's eye can fall.
(ENTER PROTEUS)
Welcome, dear Proteus! Mistress: confirm his welcome with some word.

SILVIA

His own worth speaks his welcome, if this is he of whom I've heard.

VALENTINE

Let him be my fellow servant, that as such we may both serve you.

SILVIA

Too low a mistress for so high a servant. (TO PROTEUS). I'm sure I don't deserve you.

PROTEUS

Not so, sweet lady, I'm too poor a servant to look upon a mistress so fair.
I boast only of my duty, to serve you as long as I breathe air.

(ENTER SERVANT)

SERVANT

Madam, my lord your father would speak with you anon.

SILVIA

I wait upon his pleasure. Come, Sir Turio, we must be gone.

(EXEUNT SILVIA, TURIO, SERVANT)

VALENTINE

Now tell me, how do all in Verona?

PROTEUS

Your friends and family are well.

VALENTINE

And Julia? How does your lady? How thrives your love? Pray tell!

PROTEUS

My tales of love did weary you; you joy not in such discourse.

VALENTINE

Nay, Proteus, that was before my life was altered in its course.
I've done penance for condemning Love, with nightly tears and sighs;
In revenge of my contempt, Love hath chased sleep from mine eyes.
O Proteus, Love's a mighty lord: it hath humbled me, I confess,
Till I crave no talk *except* of love.

PROTEUS
And this was she? Let me guess.

VALENTINE
Even she.

PROTEUS
When I was sick with love, you gave me bitter pills to swallow,
I must minister the like to you, now that in Love's mire you wallow.
But she loves you?

VALENTINE
Aye, we are betrothed; nay more, our marriage is set,
The cunning manner of our flight determined, all the means plotted yet:
How I must climb her window with a ladder made of cords.
Good Proteus, come to my chamber; counsel me with your words.

PROTEUS
Go on before, I shall enquire you; I must to the road to disembark,
Presently I'll attend you.

VALENTINE
Will you make haste?

PROTEUS
As Noah to the ark.
(EXIT VALENTINE)
Even as one heat expels a former heat, or one nail drives out another,
So the remembrance of my former love, this newer object will smother.
Is it mine eye or Valentine's praise that makes me reasonless to reason thus?
Her true perfection, or my false transgression that in my heart stirs such a fuss?
Silvia is fair; so is Julia that I love; that I did love, for now that love is thawed,
And like a waxen image too close to a fire, by this new heat is overawed.
Methinks my zeal to Valentine is cold, and I love him not as I did.
O, but I love his lady too much, and I cannot keep my love hid!
If I can check my erring love, I will;
If not, to win her I'll use my skill.
(EXIT)

ACT II, scene 5

(MILAN. A STREET. ENTER SPEED AND LANCE.)

SPEED
Lance, by mine honesty, welcome to Milan.

LANCE
Nay, I'm not welcome till my tavern bill be gone.

SPEED
Why you madcap, I'll to the alehouse with you, where for five pence you shall be sped.
But how did thy master part with Madam Julia? Tell me, what was said?

LANCE
After they embraced, they parted in jest.

SPEED
But shall she marry him?

LANCE
No.

SPEED
Shall he marry her?

LANCE
No.

SPEED
You put my patience to the test.
How stands the matter with them?

LANCE
When it stands well with him, it stands well with her.

SPEED
What an ass art thou! I understand thee not.

LANCE
Then *thou* art a blockhead, sir.
My staff understands me if I do but lean.

SPEED
It stands under thee, indeed.

LANCE
Stand under; understand. 'Tis all one, Master Speed.

SPEED
But tell me, will't be a match?

LANCE
Ask my dog. If he say "aye," it will.
If he say "no," it will; or if he shake his tail, he thinks it's quite a thrill.

SPEED
The conclusion then is that it will.

LANCE
Thou shalt ne'er get such a secret from me,
Unless it be by parable.

SPEED
'Tis well, for now I see.
But Lance, what say you now that *my* master is become a lover too?

LANCE
I always knew him to be a lubber. Why do I bother talking to you?

SPEED
Why, thou ass! I said "lover." You mistake me. I tell thee, my master is hot!

LANCE
Why, fool, if he burn himself in love, I tell *thee*, I care not.
Wilt thou go with me to the alehouse?

SPEED
Why?

<u>LANCE</u>
As thou say'st, to pay my bill,
That with charity thou mayst prove thyself a Christian. Wilt thou go with me?

<u>SPEED</u>
(SIGHS) I will.

(EXEUNT)

ACT II, scene 6

(MILAN. THE DUKE'S PALACE. ENTER PROTEUS.)

<u>PROTEUS</u>
To leave my Julia, shall I be forsworn;
To love fair Silvia, shall I be forsworn;
To wrong my friend is perjury threefold,
Yet Love provokes me, Love bids me be bold!
At first I did adore a twinkling star,
Now I worship the sun, brighter by far.
Who would not exchange the bad for better?
Nay, Julia is not bad. Fie! How this will upset her.
Julia I lose, and Valentine I lose
To have fair Silvia; I cannot help but choose.
In keeping them, I would lose my self,
So I must put my former oaths on a shelf,
Remembering that my love to Julia is dead,
And Valentine I must hold an enemy instead.
This night he means with a corded ladder
To climb Silvia's chamber-window like an adder.
I'll give her father notice of their intended flight,
Who, all enraged, will banish Valentine tonight,
For he intends dull Turio shall wed his daughter.
But Valentine being gone, I'll lead Turio like a lamb to slaughter.
Love, lend me wings to make my purpose swift,
As thou hast lent me wit to plot this drift.
(EXIT)

ACT II, scene 7

(VERONA. JULIA'S HOUSE. ENTER JULIA AND LUCETTA)

JULIA
Counsel, Lucetta; gentle girl, assist me now:
Teach me some good means, tell me when and how
With my honor I may undertake a journey to Milan,
To my loving Proteus; 'tis a lifetime since he's gone.

LUCETTA
Alas, the way is long, and wearisome to travel.

JULIA
A true-devoted pilgrim is not weary when she's able
To fly with Love's wings, fly to one so dear
As my gentle Proteus.

LUCETTA
Better to await his return right here.

JULIA
Know'st thou not his looks are my soul's food?
If thou but knew the touch of love, you would not be so rude.

LUCETTA
I do not seek to quench your love's hot fire,
But qualify the fire's rage, lest its extreme desire
Should burn above the bounds of reason, and you get singed.

JULIA
The more you dam it up, the more it burns!

LUCETTA
Don't come unhinged.

JULIA
Then let me go and hinder not my course to the wild ocean;
Let there be no dam to stop the current of my devotion.
Let it flow and make sweet music, giving each bright stone a kiss,
Till at last it meander to my love, and there I'll rest in bliss.

LUCETTA
But in what habit will you go along? The way is full of dangers.

JULIA
Not like a woman, for I would prevent th'encounters of lascivious strangers.
Gentle Lucetta, fit me with such weeds as beseem some gentle page.

LUCETTA
Why then your ladyship must cut your hair.

JULIA
Nay, I'll knit it up; it's all the rage.
With twenty odd-conceited love knots, I'll be a youth fantastic;
We'll tie it up with silken strings.

LUCETTA
Too bad they haven't invented elastic.
What fashion, madam, shall I make your breeches?

JULIA
Why, whatever thou likes best.

LUCETTA
You must then have a codpiece.

JULIA
Out, Lucetta! You put my patience to the test.

LUCETTA
Round hose, madam, now's not worth a pin
Unless you have a codpiece to stick pins in.

JULIA
Lucetta, as thou lov'st me, let me have what you think meet.
But how will the world repute me when, dressed so, I take to the street
In so unstaid a journey? I fear it will be a scandal.

LUCETTA
Then stay at home and go not, if you don't think you can handle
It.

JULIA
Nay, that I will not.

LUCETTA
Then go, and dream not on what will be said;
If Proteus like your journey, no matter who's displeased in his stead.
But I fear he will scarce be pleased withal.

JULIA
That is the least of my fears,
For he hath sworn a thousand oaths, and blessed them with his tears.

LUCETTA
These are servants to deceitful men.

JULIA
But truer stars governed Proteus' birth.
His words are bonds,his oaths are oracles,his faith will prove his worth.
His love is sincere, his thoughts immaculate, his tears pure messengers from his heart;
As far from fraud as heaven from earth.

LUCETTA
He's a man, so he may prove a fart.

(EXEUNT)

ACT III, scene 1

(MILAN. THE DUKE'S PALACE. ENTER DUKE, TURIO AND PROTEUS)

DUKE
Sir Turio, give us leave for a word;
We have some business.

TURIO
I will, my lord.
(EXIT)

DUKE
Now tell me, Proteus, what's your will with me?

PROTEUS
My gracious lord, as you will see,
The law of friendship bids me conceal this,
But duty pricks me on to reveal this:
Sir Valentine, my friend, this very night
Intends to steal your daughter from out your sight.
Myself am privy to the plot, and well I know
That on Turio you have determined to bestow
Her-a man your daughter hates-be that as it may,
I rather choose to cross my friend, for duty, as I say,
Compels me, so as not to give you sorrow by concealing it.

DUKE
Proteus, I thank thee for thine honest care in revealing it.
This love of theirs I have often seen,
And knowing that tender youth is green
With folly, I have nightly lodged Silvia in a tower;
Myself have kept the key to her bower,
And thence she cannot be conveyed away.

PROTEUS
My lord, Valentine has this very day
Gone to fetch a corded ladder, which he devised to fetch her down.
Her chamber-window he will ascend; tonight they will be gone.

Do but intercept him cunningly, that I be not discovered;
For love of you, not hate of him, have I this plot uncovered.

DUKE
By mine honor, he shall never know.

PROTEUS
Valentine is coming, my lord. Adieu.

(EXIT PROTEUS. ENTER VALENTINE)

DUKE
Sir Valentine, whither away so fast?

VALENTINE
Please it your grace, there's a messenger just past
That would carry my letters to my home.

DUKE
Nay, stay with me a while, now that you are come,
And I will break with thee of some affairs that touch me near:
I am resolved to take a wife. There is a lady here
Whom I affect, but my agèd eloquence she esteems not;
I would have thee be my tutor, for I have long forgot
Which way to court, how to win her sun-bright eye.

VALENTINE
Win her with gifts, more than words; a woman's mind will lie
With dumb jewels.

DUKE
She did scorn a present that I sent her.

VALENTINE
A woman sometimes scorns what best contents her.
Send her another, never give her o'er,
For scorn at first makes after-love the more.
If she do frown, 'tis not in hate of you,
But rather to beget more love in you.

DUKE
She is promised to another, and kept severely from resort of men;
No man hath access to her by day.

VALENTINE
Why, then,
I would resort to her at night.

DUKE
Her doors are locked, her chamber far from the ground.

VALENTINE
May not one enter at her window, safely without a sound?
A ladder made of cords, with a pair of anchoring hooks
Would serve to scale her tower and win her loving looks.

DUKE
Where may I have such a ladder?

VALENTINE
Pray, sir, tell me when you would use it.

DUKE
This very night, for love spurs me on; I cannot help but choose it.

VALENTINE
By seven o'clock I'll get such a ladder and bring it to you hither.

DUKE
But hark thee: I'll go to her alone; how shall I bear it thither?

VALENTINE
It will be light, my lord, that you may bear it under a cloak.

DUKE
One such as thine?

VALENTINE
Aye, my good lord.

DUKE
Let me see.

VALENTINE
You must be joking.
I mean, any cloak will serve.

DUKE
I pray thee, let me see thine.
For I would feel such a cloak upon me. Give it me, Valentine.
(TAKING VALENTINE'S CLOAK, HE FINDS A LETTER AND A LADDER)
What letter is this? "To Silvia"! I'll be so bold to break the seal.
(READS IT.) Why this is the hand of a lover, written with youthful zeal.
"Silvia, tonight will I free thee!" Why, tis so, here's the ladder for the task.
I would have given you anything but her; all you had to do was ask.
Go, base intruder, overweening slave, make thy departure hence!
After all the favors I've bestowed upon thee, this is my recompense?
If thou linger in my territories longer than the swiftest expedition,
My wrath shall far exceed my love, and swiftly seal thy perdition.
Be gone! I will not stay to hear thy vain excuse;
As you love life, make speed from hence, or reap thine own abuse.

(EXIT DUKE)

VALENTINE
And why not death, rather than living torment? Silvia is my soul!
To die would be better than banishment; without her, I'm not whole.
What light is light if Silvia be not seen? What joy is joy if Silvia be not by?
Unless to think upon the shade of her perfection, and dream that she is nigh.
She is my essence, and if I leave, I fly from her who would be my wife;
If I tarry here, I attend on death, but fly I hence, I fly from life.

(ENTER PROTEUS AND LANCE)

PROTEUS
Run, boy, run, and seek him out. What seest thou?

LANCE
Him we go to find.

PROTEUS
Valentine?

VALENTINE
No.

PROTEUS
Who then? His spirit?

VALENTINE
Nothing.

LANCE
I must be losing my mind.
Can nothing speak? Shall I strike?

PROTEUS
Strike what?

LANCE
Nothing.

PROTEUS
Villain, forbear.

LANCE
Sir, I would strike nothing.

PROTEUS
Fool, go stand over there!
Valentine, a word.

VALENTINE
My ears are stopped, and cannot hear good news,
So much of bad they have heard already; I've nothing left to lose.

LANCE
Sir, it's said you are vanished.

PROTEUS
Banished; yes that's the news.
From hence, from Silvia, from me thy friend, you must go, and cannot refuse.

VALENTINE
I have fed upon this woe already; excess will make me ill.
Doth Silvia know that I am banished?

PROTEUS
Aye, and with words most shrill,
With sighs and groans, and silver-shedding tears, she hath tendered her desire,
But none of these could penetrate her uncompassionate sire.

VALENTINE
No more, unless your next word have some power to take my life.

PROTEUS
Cease to lament. Time is the nurse will mend all woe and strife.
I'll convey you through the city gate, and even on our way there,
We will confer of all that may concern thy most chaste love affair.

VALENTINE
I pray thee, Lance, bid my boy come meet me at the North Gate.

PROTEUS
Go, sirrah, find him out. Come, Valentine, before it's too late.

(EXEUNT VALENTINE AND PROTEUS)

LANCE
I am but a fool, yet I have the wit to think my master a knave.
But that's all one; no man shall yet know *me* to be love's slave.
Yet I *am* in love; a team of horse shall not pluck from me who 'tis.
Yet 'tis a milkmaid; she hath more qualities than a water-spaniel does.
(PULLS OUT A PAPER)
Here is a list of her qualities. (READS) Item: "she can fetch and carry."
Why, a horse can do no more; nay, a horse cannot fetch, but only carry!
Item: "she can milk." Sweet virtue in a maid with clean hands.

(ENTER SPEED)

SPEED
Lance! What news with your mastership.

LANCE
My master's ship? It sails to foreign lands.

SPEED
Your old vice still: mistake the word. What news then on your paper?

LANCE
Black news.

SPEED
How black?

LANCE
As black as ink.

SPEED
Let me read this caper.
(LANCE YIELDS THE PAPER)
Item: "she can milk."

LANCE
That she can.

SPEED
Item: "she brews good ale."
Item: "she can knit and spin."

LANCE
And thereby hangs a tale.

SPEED
I see her virtues, what of her vices?

LANCE
They follow at virtue's heels.

SPEED
"She must not eat on account of her breath."

LANCE
She doesn't brush between meals.

SPEED
"She talks in her sleep."

LANCE
No matter for that, if she sleeps not in her talk.

SPEED

"She is slow in words."

LANCE

This is not a vice. Villain! Why do you mock?
To be slow in words is a woman's only virtue.

SPEED

Item: "She is proud."

LANCE

Out with that too! She may be slow, but at least she isn't loud.

SPEED

"She hath no teeth:

LANCE

I care not for that because I love to eat the crust.

SPEED

"She is curst."

LANCE

But she hath no teeth to bite! This item is a must.

SPEED

"She will often praise her liquor."

LANCE

If her liquor be good, so will I.

SPEED

"She is too liberal."

LANCE

Faith, she's not running for office. Fie!

SPEED

"She hath more hair than wit, more faults than hairs, and more wealth than her faults."

LANCE
Stop right there! More wealth? I'll have her! I'll do summersaults!
Thy master stays for thee at the North Gate.

SPEED
My master? Why didst thou not tell me before?

(HE RETURNS THE LETTER.EXIT SPEED.)

LANCE
(READS) "More wealth than faults." Hmm. I want her more and more.
(EXIT)

ACT III, scene 2

(ENTER DUKE AND TURIO)

DUKE
Sir Turio, fear not; she'll love you now that Valentine is banished.

TURIO
Since his exile, the little warmth she used to show me has vanished.
She hath despised me, railed at me, forsworn my sight,
I am desperate of obtaining her with all my might.

DUKE
A little time will melt her frozen thought,
And worthless Valentine shall be forgot.
(ENTER PROTEUS)
How now, Sir Proteus: is your countryman gone, according to my will?

PROTEUS
Gone, my lord.

DUKE
My daughter takes his going grievously still.

PROTEUS
A little time, my lord, will kill that grief.

DUKE
So believe I; *that* will be a relief.
Thou know'st how willingly I would effect the match
Between my daughter and Sir Turio; he's quite a catch.
And also thou art not ignorant, methinks,
How she opposes my will, the ungrateful minx.

PROTEUS
She did, my lord, when Valentine was here.

DUKE
And perversely maintains, that much is clear.
What might we do to make the girl forget
The love of Valentine, and love Turio yet?

PROTEUS
The best way is with slander; to speak ill of her former lover.

DUKE
She'll think it is spoke in hate.

SIR TURIO
And then we'd best run for cover.

PROTEUS
If an enemy deliver it, she may rail,
But if spoken by a friend, it cannot fail.

DUKE
Then *you* must undertake it, if what you say is true.

PROTEUS
And that, my lord, I shall be loathe to do.

DUKE
Your slander can never damage him in the end,
Being entreated to it by one who is your friend.

PROTEUS
You have prevailed, my lord. She shall not continue to love him.
But it follows not that Sir Turio will then stand above him.

SIR TURIO
Therefore, while from him you do unwind her love,
You must wrap it on me, so that I may find her love.
You must praise me as much as your friend you dispraise,
Which shouldn't be hard; one has only to gaze
Upon me to see which of us is better.

DUKE
Proteus, we trust that you won't upset her.
Upon this warrant you shall have access to her,
To temper her by persuasion, and for this man, woo her.

PROTEUS
But you, Sir Turio, must angle for her love
With wailful sonnets cast to her above.

Say that upon the altar of her beauty
You sacrifice your heart.

SIR TURIO
She *is* a cutie.

PROTEUS
Visit your lady's chamber window by night,
With lamenting elegies sung out of sight.
By this, and nothing else, you will inherit her.

SIR TURIO
I'll do it, this very night! God knows, I merit her.
Therefore, sweet Proteus, my direction-giver,
Let us into the city; I'm all a-quiver!
We'll find some gentleman who in music is skilled,
I have a sonnet that will serve; Silvia will be thrilled!

PROTEUS
We'll wait upon your grace after supper, do not doubt it.

DUKE
I pardon you, gentlemen. About it, now, about it!

(EXEUNT)

ACT IV, scene 1

(A FOREST NEAR MILAN. ENTER THREE OUTLAWS)

<u>OUTLAW 1</u>
Fellows, stand fast. I see a stranger.

<u>OUTLAW 2</u>
If there be ten, shrink not from danger.

(ENTER VALENTINE AND SPEED)

<u>OUTLAW 3</u>
Stand, sir, and throw us what you have in your possession,
Or else we'll make you sit, and help ourselves at our discretion!

<u>VALENTINE</u>
My friends …

<u>OUTLAW 1</u>
That's not so, sir; we are your enemies this day!

<u>OUTLAW 2</u>
Peace! Let him speak. We'll hear what he has to say.

<u>OUTLAW 3</u>
Aye, by my beard we will, for he is a proper youth.

<u>VALENTINE</u>
Then know that these poor clothes are all I have, that's the truth.

<u>OUTLAW 1</u>
Whither travel you?

<u>VALENTINE</u>
To Verona.

<u>OUTLAW 2</u>
Whence came you?

VALENTINE
From Milan.

OUTLAW 3
How long stayed you there?

VALENTINE
Some sixteen months, until I was forced to move on.

OUTLAW 1
What, were you banished thence?

VALENTINE
I was.

OUTLAW 2
You don't say. So was I.

OUTLAW 3
For what offence?

SPEED
He killed a man. He's not just a regular guy.

OUTLAW 1
But were you banished for so small a fault?

VALENTINE
I was. In truth, for less.

OUTLAW 2
Speak you languages?

VALENTINE
One or two.

SPEED
Seven! Master, confess.

OUTLAW 3
This fellow were a king for us!

OUTLAW 1
We'll have him.

OUTLAW 2
Sirs, a word.

(THE OUTLAWS DELIBERATE)

SPEED
Master, I pray you, be one of them.

VALENTINE
Are you mad? Don't be absurd.

OUTLAW 3
Know, sir, that some of us are gentlemen, who in the fury of our youthful days
Have done such deeds as you yourself, and so found this life.

OUTLAW 1
It pays.

OUTLAW 2
Because you are a banished man, above others we parley with you.
Are you content to be our general, and live in this wilderness too?

OUTLAW 3
Say "aye," and be our captain. We'll do thee homage and be ruled by thee.

OUTLAW 1
But if you say "no" and scorn our courtesy, we'll have to kill you.

VALENTINE
I see.
I take your offer and will live with you.

SPEED
So will I! He can't live without me.

VALENTINE
(TO OUTLAWS) Provided you do no outrages on women.

<u>OUTLAW 2</u>
We despise such villains, do not doubt me.

<u>OUTLAW 3</u>
Come, go with us, we'll bring you to our crews,
And show you our treasure; all is at your dispose.

(EXEUNT)

ACT IV, scene 2

(MILAN. OUTSIDE SILVIA'S WINDOW. ENTER PROTEUS)

PROTEUS
Already have I been false to Valentine, now Turio I must mislead;
But Silvia is too holy to be corrupted with this deed.
She twits me with my falsehood to Valentine, my friend;
She bids me think of Julia when her own beauty I commend.
Yet spaniel-like, I follow her; my lover's hope governs my will;
The more she spurns me, the more it grows, and fawneth on her still.

(ENTER TURIO AND MUSICIANS)

TURIO
How now, Sir Proteus, are you crept here before us?

PROTEUS
Love will creep where it cannot go.

TURIO
I hope, sir, you love not Silvia.

PROTEUS
I do, for your sake, Turio.

TURIO
I thank you. Gentlemen, let's tune, and to it lustily awhile,

(ENTER HOST OF THE INN AND JULIA, *DISGUISED AS SEBASTIAN, A PAGE*)

HOST
Now, my young guest, methinks you're melancholy. I long to see you smile.

JULIA
Mine host, I cannot be merry.

HOST
I'll bring you where you shall her a tune,
And see the gentleman you asked for.

JULIA
Shall I see him soon?
And hear him speak? For that will be music.

HOST
Hark, they begin to play!

(PRELUDE TO THE SONG BEGINS)

JULIA
Is he among these?

HOST
Aye; but peace, let's hear 'em. He will shortly come this way.

SONG
Who is Silvia? What is she, that all our swains commend her?
Holy, fair and wise is she; the heaven such grace did lend her
That she might admirèd be.

Is she kind as she is fair? For Beauty lives with Kindness.
Love doth to her eyes repair to help him of his blindness,
And being helped, inhabits there.

Then to Silvia let us sing that Silvia is excelling;
She excels each mortal thing upon the dull earth dwelling
And to her let us garlands bring.

HOST
Methinks the music likes you not. Are you sadder than before?

JULIA
Methinks that musician likes me not, to be standing at this lady's door.
But Host, doth this Sir Proteus we talk on, resort often to this venue?

HOST
Lance, his man, hath told me that Silvia is the favorite item on his menu.

PROTEUS
Sir Turio, fear you not; I will with all cunning plead.

TURIO
Where meet we?

PROTEUS
At St. Gregory's Well.

TURIO
Hasten there with speed.

(EXEUNT TURIO AND MUSICIANS. SILVIA ENTERS ABOVE)

SILVIA
Who's there?

PROTEUS
Good even to your ladyship.

SILVIA
I thank you for your song.

PROTEUS
If you knew my pure heart's truth, you would know me by voice 'ere long.

SILVIA
Sir Proteus, I take it.

PROTEUS
Gentle lady, your servant.

SILVIA
What's your will?

PROTEUS
To compass your own.

SILVIA
My will is this: that presently you hie thee home!
Thou subtle, false, disloyal man; think you that I am so young,
To be seduced by flattery, deceived by thy vows; wooed by songs you have sung?
Return, return, make thy *own* love amends; sing to *her* instead.

PROTEUS
I grant, sweet love, I did love a lady once, but I hear that she is dead.

JULIA
(ASIDE) 'Twere false if I should speak it, for I'm sure she is not buried.

SILVIA
Yet Valentine lives; thy friend, to whom I am to be married.

PROTEUS
I likewise hear that Valentine is dead.

SILVIA
Then so am I, for my love goes to his grave.
Go! Hasten to thy lady's tomb, and pray her love may yet save
You.

PROTEUS
If you will not give your heart, at least grant me something of thine,
Your picture: I'll sigh and weep to it, if you'll vouchsafe it may be mine.

SILVIA
I am loathe to be your idol; but since falsehood becomes you so well,
I'll send it for you to worship, as you pave your road to Hell.

(EXIT SEPARTELY SILVIA AND PROTEUS)

JULIA
Host, will you go?

HOST
Faith, gentle sir, I was fast asleep.

JULIA
Pray, take me to my lodging, that I may go there and weep.

(EXEUNT)

ACT IV, scene 3

(MILAN. OUTSIDE SILVIA'S HOUSE. ENTER EGLAMOUR)

EGLAMOUR
This is the hour Madam Silvia bid me come, her wishes to make clear;
There's some great matter she'd employ me in. Madam! Sir Eglamour is here!

(ENTER SILVIA)

SILVIA
Sir Eglamour, a thousand times good morrow.

EGLAMOUR
I attend your ladyship's command.
I am come to know your pleasure; what danger is close at hand?

SILVIA
Sir Eglamour, thou art a gentleman; valiant, accomplished and wise.
You know what love I bear Valentine; my father would give me as prize
To vain Turio. You have loved. Thy grief was great when thy lady died;
O Eglamour, I would to Valentine! But the road is long and wide,
It's dangerous to pass; I do desire thy company, upon whose faith I trust.
If you will not, I'll depart alone in haste, for go I must.

EGLAMOUR
Madam, I pity much your grief, which I know is virtuously placed.
I give consent to go with you, that your virtue may not be disgraced.
When will you go?

SILVIA
This evening coming.

EGLAMOUR
Where shall I meet you?

SILVIA
At Friar Patrick's cell.

EGLAMOUR
I will not fail your ladyship.

SILVIA
Kind Sir Eglamour, farewell.

(EXIT SEPARATELY)

ACT IV, scene 4

(ENTER LANCE WITH HIS DOG)

LANCE
(POINTING TO HIS DOG)
When a man's servant plays the cur with him, see how it brings disaster:
I was sent to deliver a present to Mistress Silvia from my master;
Crab thrusts himself into the company of gentleman-like dogs under the Duke's table,
And had not been there a pissing while when all the chamber smelt like a stable!
"Out with the dog!" says one. "What dog?" says another, "Whip him out!"
I, being acquainted with this smell, knew it was *this* lout,
So goes me to the fellow and say, "Friend, you do him wrong;
'Twas I did the thing you smell." So he whips *me* out 'ere long.
How many masters would do this for a servant? (TO CRAB) Thou think'st not of this now.
I have sat in the stocks for puddings he has stolen; once he tried to milk a cow! (TO CRAB) When I took leave of Madam Silvia, did I not bid thee do as I do? When did you see *me* heave up my leg against a lady and make water on her shoe?

(ENTER PROTEUS AND JULIA, *DISGUISED AS SEBASTIAN*)

PROTEUS
Sebastian is thy name? I like thee well, and will in some service employ thee.

JULIA
In what you please; I'll do what I can.

PROTEUS
(INDICATING LANCE) Not like *this* one, who would annoy me.
How now, you peasant, where have you been loitering for these two days?

LANCE
I carried Mistress Silvia the dog you bade me; sir, I am not lazy.

PROTEUS
And what says she to my little jewel?

LANCE
She says she will not have a cur from a fool.

PROTEUS
She received not my dog?

LANCE
No, indeed. Here have I brought him back.

PROTEUS
(POINTS TO CRAB) Didst thou offer her *this* from me?

LANCE
Aye, for that squirrel you bid me pack
Was stolen by boys in the market place, so I offered her mine own,
He's bigger than yours, therefore the greater gift. He even came with a bone.

PROTEUS
Go, get thee hence, and find my dog, or ne'er return to my sight!
Away, I say!

LANCE
I'm going. (ASIDE) It's a pity I never trained Crab to bite.

(EXIT LANCE WITH CRAB)

PROTEUS
Sebastian, I have entertained thee partly that I have need of a youth
That with some discretion can do my business, for as you've seen in truth,
There is no trusting yond foolish lout. Therefore I'll entrust thee:
Deliver this ring to Madam Silvia; one who loved me well gave it to *me*.

JULIA
It seems you loved not her, to part with her token. Is she dead?

PROTEUS
Not so.

JULIA
Alas!

PROTEUS
Wherefore "alas"?

JULIA
I can't help but pity her instead.
Methinks she loved you as you love Silvia, who loves not you.
'Tis pity love should be so contrary; thinking on it makes me blue.

PROTEUS
Give her this ring, and tell her I claim the promise of her heavenly picture;
Then come to my chamber, where you shall find me like a monk at his scripture.

(EXIT PROTEUS)

JULIA
How many women would do such a message? Alas, why do I pity?
This ring I gave *him* when he parted from me and came unto this city.
(ENTER SILVIA, WITH ATTENDANTS)
Gentlewoman, good day. Pray bring me where I may speak with the Duke's
daughter.

SILVIA
Who are you? For I am she.

JULIA
(ASIDE) And I'm a lamb led to slaughter.
(TO SILVIA) Sir Proteus, sends me for a picture.

SILVIA
Ursula, bring it here.
(ONE OF THE ATTENDANTS FETCHES THE PORTRAIT)
Give your master this from me, one he claims to hold dear.
Tell him a portrait of the lady Julia, whom his changing thoughts forget,
Would better fit his chamber; he does her much wrong yet.

JULIA
She thanks you.

SILVIA
Dost thou know her?

JULIA
Almost as well as myself.

SILVIA
Belike she thinks Proteus forsook her?

JULIA
She doth feel herself put on some shelf.

SILVIA
Is she not passing fair?

JULIA
She hath been fairer, madam, when my master loved her well,
As fair as you, in my judgment, before he fell under your spell.

SILVIA
Alas, poor lady! Here, good youth, take my purse, for thy mistress' sake,
Because thou lov'st her. And so, farewell.

(EXIT SILVIA AND ATTENDANTS)

JULIA
I think I've made a mistake:
This is a virtuous gentlewoman, mild and full of grace!
I hope my master's suit will be cold, since she respects my mistress's place!
(EXIT)

ACT V, scene 1

(MILAN. FRIAR PATRICK'S CELL. ENTER EGLAMOUR)

EGLAMOUR

The sun begins to gild the western sky; now is the very hour
That Silvia should meet me at Friar Patrick's cell, with only her love for a
dower.
She will not fail; lovers break not their time, unless to come before it,
So much do they spur their expedition. Ah, love! You can't ignore it.
See where she comes. Lady, happy evening.

SILVIA

Good Eglamour, amen.
I fear I'm attended by spies; by the abbey I saw some men.

EGLAMOUR

Fear not, the forest is but three leagues off; if we reach that, we are sure.
No man may harm you whilst in my company, or my name isn't Eglamour!

(EXEUNT)

ACT V, scene 2

(MILAN. THE DUKE'S PALACE. ENTER TURIO, PROTEUS AND JULIA, *DISGUISED AS SEBASTIAN*)

TURIO
Sir Proteus, tell me, what says Silvia to my suit?

PROTEUS
She says your leg is too little.

TURIO
Why, then, I'll wear a boot.
What says she to my face?

PROTEUS
She says it is a fair one.

TURIO
And to my valor?

PROTEUS
O, she says that you're a rare one.

JULIA
(ASIDE) Which is another way of saying that she knows thee for a coward.

TURIO
Likes she my discourse?

PROTEUS
Not well. Your talk of war has soured
Her.

(ENTER DUKE)

JULIA
Here comes the duke.

DUKE
How now, gentlemen; saw you Sir Eglamour of late?

TURIO
Not I.

PROTEUS
Nor I.

DUKE
Saw you my daughter within the city gate?

PROTEUS
Not since last night.

DUKE
Why then she's fled unto that peasant Valentine,
And Eglamour in her company; they were seen tonight at nine.
I pray you, mount, and presently meet me on the rising slope
Of the mountain that leads toward Mantua, to catch them before there's no hope.
Dispatch, gentlemen, and follow.

(EXIT DUKE)

TURIO
Why, this is a peevish girl,
I'll after, more to be revenged on Eglamour than for love of this feckless churl.

(EXIT TURIO)

PROTEUS
And I will follow, more for Silvia's love than hate of Eglamour.

(EXIT PROTEUS)

JULIA
And I'll follow to cross that love, though why, I'm not quite sure.
(EXIT)

ACT V, scene 3

(THE FOREST NEAR MILAN. ENTER SILVIA AND THREE OUTLAWS)

OUTLAW 1
Be patient, we must bring you to our captain.

SILVIA
Mischance hath taught me worse than this may yet happen.

OUTLAW 2
Where is the gentleman that with this lady did start?

OUTLAW 3
Escaped into the wood; he's a nimble old fart.

OUTLAW 2
Let us follow. Go thou to the west end of the wood.

(EXEUNT OUTLAWS 2 & 3)

OUTLAW 1
Come, to our captain's cave.

SILVIA
I fear it will bring me to no good.

OUTLAW 1
Fear not, he bears an honorable mind, and will not use a woman lawlessly.

SILVIA
O, Valentine, what I endure for loving thee so flawlessly!

(EXEUNT)

ACT V, scene 4

(THE FOREST. ENTER VALENTINE)

<u>VALENTINE</u>
How use doth breed a habit in a man!
This wood I better brook than peopled town.
Here can I sit alone, unseen of any,
And to the nightingale's tune, count my woes to the penny.
Repair me with thy presence, Silvia, my own;
Thou gentle nymph, cherish thy forlorn swain.
(SHOUTS AND SOUNDS OF FIGHTING)
What halloing and what stir is this today?
My mates and some unhappy passenger come this way.
I have much to do to keep them from uncivil 'havior;
But who comes here? A lady and her savior.

(VALENTINE STEPS ASIDE. ENTER PROTEUS, SILVIA AND JULIA, *AS SEBASTIAN*)

<u>PROTEUS</u>
Madam, I have risked both life and limb;
You respect it not, I rescued you from him
That would have forced your love and honor.
Vouchsafe me one fair look, or I'm a goner.

<u>SILVIA</u>
O miserable, unhappy that I am.
Do you think your coming pleased me, Proteus; you ham!
Had I been seized by a hungry lion, I would *rather*
Have been breakfast to the beast than hear your blather!
O heaven be judge how I love Valentine,
And do detest Proteus! You shall never be mine!

<u>PROTEUS</u>
Then I will woo you like a soldier, by the sword,
And force your love, for I will be your lord.
(HE LAYS HANDS UPON HER)

VALENTINE
(COMING FORWARD) Ruffian, let go that rude uncivil touch!
Thou friend of ill fashion! Treacherous man, you have much
Beguiled my hopes. Nought but mine own eye
Could have persuaded me you were such a scumbag. Why?
O, Proteus, now I dare not say I have one friend;
You are perjured. You, whom I had trusted to the end.
The private wound is deepest. O time accurst!
Amongst all foes that a friend should be the worst!

PROTEUS
My shame and guilt confounds me. Forgive me, dear friend.
If hearty sorrow be sufficient ransom, let me make amends.
I ask thee, Valentine, from the depths of my heart,
Raise up your fallen comrade; let him make a new start.

VALENTINE
Then I receive thee once more as an honest friend.
Time will heal the wounds, and there's an end.
And that my love may appear plain and free,
All that was mine in Silvia, I give thee.

JULIA
O me unhappy!
(SWOONS)

PROTEUS
Look to the boy.

VALENTINE
How now? Why, wag, do you toy
With us? What's the matter? Can you speak? Pray, let your voice sing.

JULIA
O good sir: my master charged me to deliver this ring;
I was to give it to Madam Silvia, but failed in my employ.

PROTEUS
Why, this is the ring I gave Julia. Where did you get it, boy?

JULIA
Julia gave it me. (DISCOVERS HERSELF) And Julia herself hath brought it hither.

PROTEUS
How? Julia?

SILVIA
(ASIDE) See how Love doth make the fool within him wither.

JULIA
O Proteus, let this habit make you blush.

PROTEUS
Is it you?

JULIA
In a disguise of love. To have you is my only wish.

PROTEUS
What was in Silvia's face but I may spy
More fresh in Julia's with a constant eye?

VALENTINE
Come, a hand from either, let me be blessed to make this happy close;
It were a pity that two such friends should long be foes.

(ENTER DUKE, TURIO, AND OUTLAWS, WITH EGLAMOUR, SPEED, LANCE WITH CRAB, AND OTHERS)

OUTLAWS
A prize, a prize, a prize!

VALENTINE
Forbear! This is my lord the Duke.
Your grace is welcome. I am banished Valentine.

TURIO
Valentine! You make me puke.
Silvia's mine.

VALENTINE
Turio, give back, or else embrace thy death.
Do not name Silvia thine, nor let thy foul breath
So much as touch her. Come not within the measure of my wrath.

LANCE
My dog is angry too.

SPEED
Turio: do the math.

(TURIO SEES HIMSELF SURROUNDED)

TURIO
I care not for her; I hold him but a a fool that will endanger
His body for a girl that loves him not; to me she's a stranger.
I claim her not, Valentine, and therefore she is thine.

DUKE
The more degenerate, thou. Sir Turio, you're a swine;
To make such means for her as thou hast done,
Then on such slight conditions, turn and run.
Valentine, I do applaud thy spirit,
And proclaim here so that all can hear it:
I cancel all grudge in favor of thy unrivalled merit.
I think thee worthy of an empress' love, and thou should bear it.
Take thou thy Silvia, for you have deserved her;
From the hands of lesser men you have conserved her.

VALENTINE
This gift makes me happy. I now beseech your grace,
Grant me one boon: the banished men of this place,
Are endowed with worthy qualities; I bid you set them free.

DUKE
Dispose of them as you wish. I pardon them and thee.
Come, let us go, we will end all enmity
With triumphs, mirth, and rare solemnity.

VALENTINE

Come, Proteus, 'tis your penance but to hear
The story of your loves discovered, both far and near.
That done, our day of marriage shall be thine:
One feast, one house, one happiness divine.

(EXEUNT ALL BUT LANCE AND CRAB)

LANCE

'Tis said each man must have his mate, and every dog his day.
I know not, but if Crab could talk, here's what he might say:
"Man thinks himself the master, of woman, cat and cur;
They know too well his folly, and yet they do prefer
To live with man, nor live alone; they pity him, I think;
Each man has good within him, but even a good man can be a fink."
Ah, well: we have our better parts, yet I would not contradict my Crab:
He has the soul of a poet, though outside he be but drab.
So let your hearts forgive our sins, and let the sound take flight,
So with your gentle hands bid our good players a good night.

<u>CURTAIN</u>

About the Author—
RICHARD CARTER

Richard Carter grew up in Portland, Oregon, the son of a doctor and a dancer. Since 1986 he has made his home in the San Juan Islands, between the Olympic Peninsula and mainland of Washington State.

After graduating from Vassar College and receiving his MFA in playwriting from the University of Washington, Richard's play *Blood and Iron* won the 1993 Jumpstart New Play Competition and was presented by the Seattle Shakespeare Company, and then on the London stage. His musical play, *Winds in the Morning*, received glowing reviews in at the 1997 Seattle Fringe Festival, and was selected to inaugurate the Wooden Boat Festival in 2000, at Port Townsend, Washington.

Richard offers his talents in many venues. As Co-Founder/Director of the Community Shakespeare Company, Richard is one of the few playwrights today with the audacity to work *with* Shakespeare. Working in rhyming couplets, updating some of the language, he delivers the best of the Bard for performance by young actors. The adaptations are so authentic that audiences scarcely know they aren't seeing and hearing the original.

Community Shakespeare Company itself breaks new ground. Its mission, "to enrich young lives and cultivate community" uses Shakespeare as the inspiration, and theatre as the means. Richard's unique adaptations motivate and enchant young actors from 3rd grade up. His leadership skills engage parents, mentors and artists to support and encourage their youth. The result is a dynamic model that can be replicated in schools, organizations, clubs and communities.

Richard and his wife Jeanna live on a small farm where they have been raising children and practicing sustainable agriculture together since 1988.

978-0-595-45825-7
0-595-45825-4

Printed in the United States
123628LV00004B/1-3/A

9 780595 458257